EDGE BOOKS

DRAWING COOL STUFF

HOW TO DRAW

MANGA WARRIORS

by Aaron Sautter

illustrated by Cynthia Martin

Capstone
press

Mankato, Minnesota

Edge Books are published by Capstone Press,
151 Good Counsel Drive, P.O. Box 669, Mankato, Minnesota 56002.
www.capstonepress.com

Library of Congress Cataloging-in-Publication Data
Sautter, Aaron.
    How to draw manga warriors / by Aaron Sautter ; illustrated by Cynthia Martin.
    p. cm.—(Edge books. Drawing cool stuff)
    Includes bibliographical references and index.
    Summary: "Lively text and fun illustrations describe how to draw manga
warriors"—Provided by publisher.
    ISBN–13: 978-1-4296-0078-1 (hardcover)
    ISBN–10: 1-4296-0078-0 (hardcover)
    1. Heroes in art—Juvenile literature. 2. Comic books, strips, etc.—Japan—
Technique. 3. Cartooning—Technique—Juvenile literature. I. Martin, Cynthia, 1961–
II. Title. III. Series.
NC1764.8.H47S282 2008
741.5—dc22   2007003454

Credits
Jason Knudson, designer

TABLE OF CONTENTS

WELCOME!

You probably picked this book because you love manga. Or maybe you picked it because you like to draw. Whatever the reason, get ready to dive into the world of manga warriors!

Thousands of manga comics are published every year around the world. Warriors are some of the most popular characters in manga. From honorable samurai to ninja spies and huge warrior robots, there are hundreds of manga warriors you can draw.

This book is just a starting point. Once you've learned how to draw the mighty warriors in this book, you can start drawing your own. Let your imagination run wild, and see what kinds of fantastic manga warriors you can create!

To get started, you'll need some supplies:

1. First you'll need drawing paper. Any type of blank, unlined paper will do.

2. Pencils are the easiest to use for your drawing projects. Make sure you have plenty of them.

3. You have to keep your pencils sharp to make clean lines. Keep a pencil sharpener close by. You'll use it a lot.

4. As you practice drawing, you'll need a good eraser. Pencil erasers wear out very fast. Get a rubber or kneaded eraser. You'll be glad you did.

5. When your drawing is finished, you can trace over it with a black ink pen or thin felt-tip marker. The dark lines will really make your work stand out.

6. If you decide to color your drawings, colored pencils and markers usually work best. You can also use colored pencils to shade your drawings and make them more lifelike.

JAD

Faces are important when drawing manga. Large eyes, small noses, and pointed chins are common in most manga characters. Facial expressions show how a character feels. Here you can see that Jad isn't happy.

When you're done with this drawing, try giving Jad some different facial expressions.

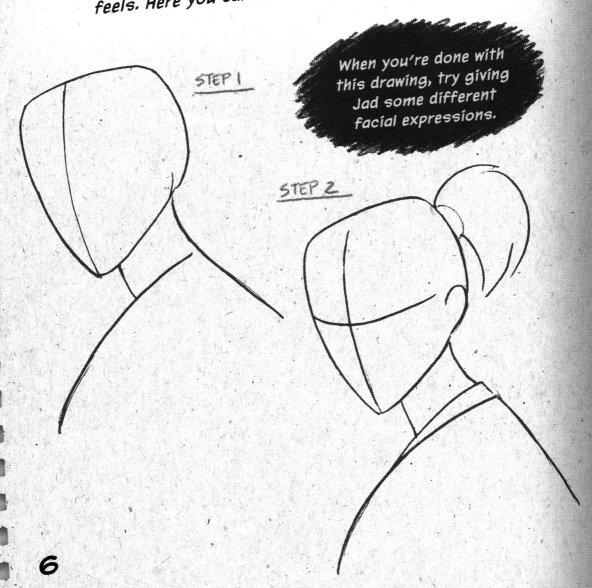

STEP 1

STEP 2

STEP 3

STEP 4

FINAL!

7

SARYNA

Saryna's eyes are larger than Jad's. They show even more emotion. Her face is rounder, and her nose is smaller too. Her frowning eyebrows and unhappy mouth show she's upset about something.

After practicing this drawing, try giving Saryna some different hairstyles or facial expressions.

STEP 1

STEP 2

STEP 3

STEP 4

FINAL!

9

KARATE PRACTICE

Like most warriors, Jad practices his martial arts skills daily. His powerful arms and swift karate moves can defend almost any attack. He wants to have the fastest hands in the land.

When you're done with this drawing, try having Jad practice some powerful karate punches!

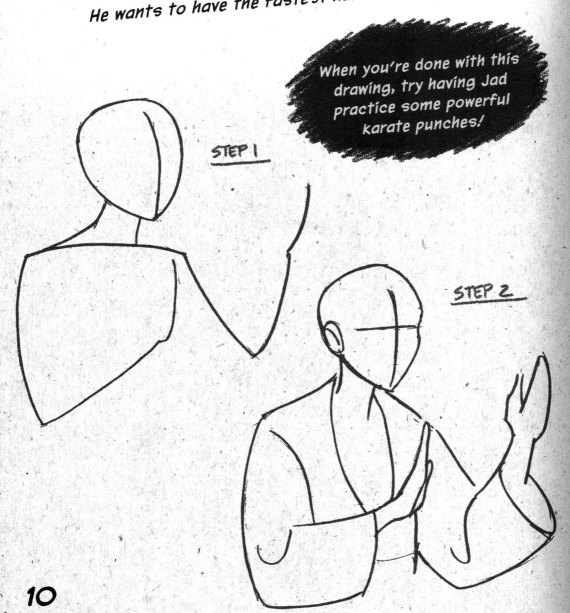

STEP 1

STEP 2

STEP 3

FINAL!

SWORD PRACTICE

Saryna hopes to one day be a mighty hero like her father. She has chosen a katana sword to help defend her village. She isn't as strong or fast as Jad, but she is deadly with a weapon in her hands.

When you've finished this drawing, try having Saryna strike a new pose with her sword!

STEP 1

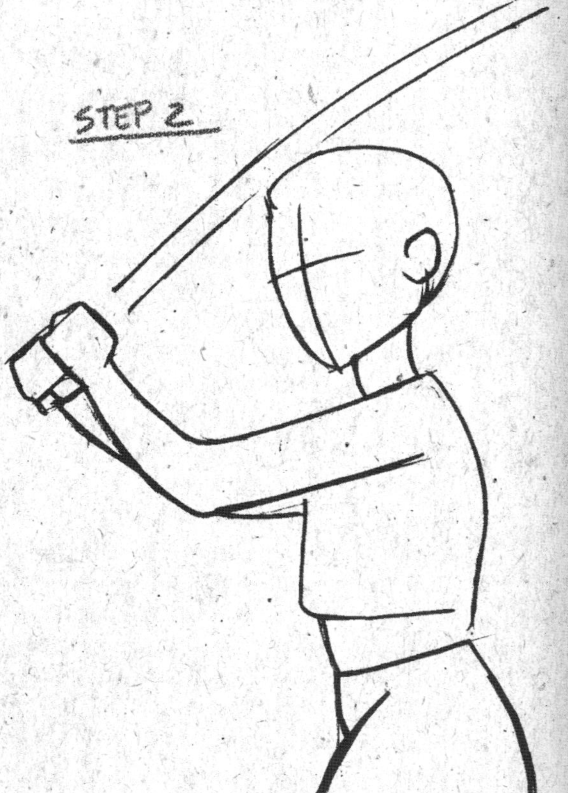

STEP 2

STEP 3

STEP 4

FINAL!

13

HIROTO

Through many years of practice and lots of hard work, Hiroto became a martial arts master. When faced with danger, he can defeat enemies in the blink of an eye. His fierceness and speed are legendary in his homeland.

When you've mastered this drawing, try giving Hiroto some ninjas to fight against!

STEP 1

STEP 2

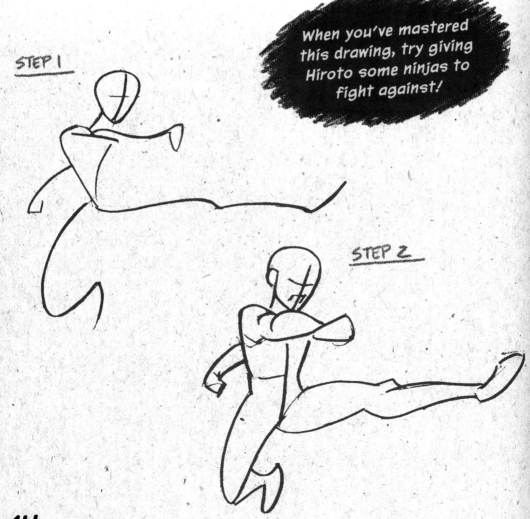

STEP 3

STEP 4

FINAL!

15

LINWEYA

Linweya has worked hard to become a master of the sword. She is a deadly foe with any blade. Luckily, she only uses her talents to defend the innocent. Like Hiroto, the people of her homeland are awed by her heroic deeds.

Once you've practiced this drawing, try giving Linweya some warriors to battle against!

STEP 1

STEP 2

STEP 3

STEP 4

FINAL!

17

MARAGI

Maragi is old—very old. Legends say he was once an evil wizard. As punishment, he was cursed to live forever. Now he teaches his students the honorable ways of the warrior code. He hopes to one day be released from his curse and finally be at rest.

STEP 1

After practicing this drawing, try showing Maragi teaching new moves to a young warrior!

STEP 2

STEP 3

STEP 4

FINAL!

19

YUNA

Yuna is one of Maragi's best students. She is strong-willed, and often disobeys her parents. But with Maragi's teaching, Yuna is quickly becoming a highly skilled fighter. She is especially talented with her favorite weapon—the nunchucku.

When you're done with this drawing, try giving Yuna some new moves to use with her nunchucks!

STEP 1

STEP 2

STEP 3

STEP 4

FINAL!

21

GENERAL KUROK

The ways of the warrior will continue in the future. In the year 2235, General Kurok commands the battleship Blazing Arkon. Through studying history's greatest warriors, he has become the mightiest commander to ever travel the stars.

STEP 1

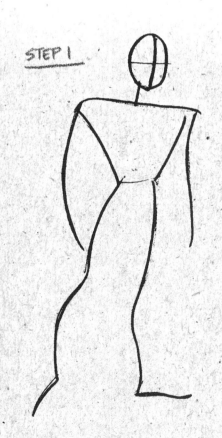

After you've practiced this drawing, try creating your own armor for General Kurok to wear!

STEP 2

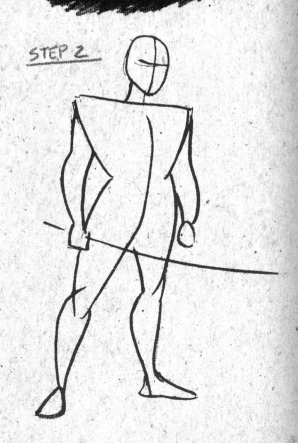

STEP 3

STEP 4

FINAL!

23

GHINSHU

Ghinshu is a master of the blade. He has fought in many battles in many lands. His body bears many scars, and he recently lost an eye battling a skilled foe. But in spite of his reduced vision, Ghinshu remains a deadly fighter with his sword.

After drawing Ghinshu, try drawing him again dueling another warrior!

STEP 1

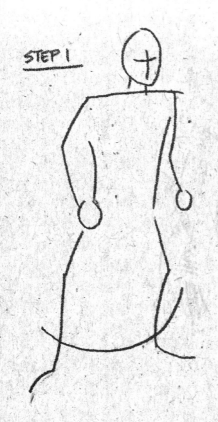

STEP 2

STEP 3

STEP 4

FINAL!

25

EPIC BATTLES

The Warriors of the Crescent Moon long fought against all injustice and evil. But one day the Black Emperor sent his emissary to dispose of those who stood against him. The epic battles between the warriors and the Black Emissary later became the stuff of legend.

This is just one possible scene from this battle. After you've drawn it, try your own poses and moves for these mortal enemies!

STEP 1

TO FINISH THIS DRAWING,
TURN TO THE NEXT PAGE!

28

STEP 6

FINAL!

29

GLOSSARY

emmissary (EM-uh-sayr-ee)—an agent or representative of a powerful person

epic (EP-ik)—heroic, or impressive; epic stories include large battles and many adventures.

karate (kah-RAH-tee)—a martial art using controlled kicks and punches

katana (kah-TAH-nah)—a curved, single-edged sword used by samurai warriors

manga (MAHN-guh)—a type of comic book or graphic novel from Japan

ninja (NIN-juh)—someone who is highly trained in Japanese martial arts and stealth; ninja were often used as spies.

nunchucku (nuhn-CHAH-koo)—an ancient oriental weapon made from two sticks joined by a chain or thick cord

samurai (SAH-muh-rye)—a skilled Japanese warrior who served one master or leader

READ MORE

Hart, Christopher. *Kids Draw Manga*. Kids Draw. New York: Watson-Guptill, 2004.

Okum, David. *Manga Madness*. Cincinnati: Impact Books, 2006.

Top That!, ed. *Ninja Warriors*. How to Draw Manga. Valencia, Cal.: Top That! Kids, 2005.

INTERNET SITES

FactHound offers a safe, fun way to find Internet sites related to this book. All of the sites on FactHound have been researched by our staff.

Here's how:
1. Visit *www.facthound.com*
2. Choose your grade level.
3. Type in this book ID code **1429600780** for age-appropriate sites. You may also browse subjects by clicking on letters, or by clicking on pictures and words.
4. Click on the **Fetch It** button.

FactHound will fetch the best sites for you!

INDEX